Reach for me when…

Kazbano Ali Kalhoro

BookLeaf Publishing

India | USA | UK

Presentation by *BookLeaf Publishing*

Web: www.bookleafpub.com

E-mail: info@bookleafpub.com

ISBN: 9789357445412

First edition 2021

DEDICATION

Worlds beautiful people

ACKNOWLEDGEMENT

For the inspiration of these poems I have to thank life and bitterness of reality, as real life events are what my poems are based on further more i have Failure to thank because if I wasn't failing in my first college i would of never taken that step to put pen to paper which lead to the discovery that I can write poems.
Kazbano Ali kalhoro

PREFACE

This book is fill with variety of emotive and intense poems ready to strike the cords of your heart .

Dear lover

Dear lover I want you to love my soul
Over my body
Love my being over my Beaty
Love me for me
Dear lover if you love me
Tell me that one day
this Love will sale us so far away
From the normal peoples land
I want to get lost with you so far away
People will watch in awe and think we fell
astray
When I'm fact Astray is for them not me
As my eyes are the key to your soul
I want to set you free
Free
Free like the birds
Free
Free like the breez
Free but you'll still chose me
And that is the Beaty of love
All your life
your soul is caged within a body made of flesh
and blood
After me

Your soul chooses to reside with me for all of
Eternity
But in the case dear lover
The sweet sound of freedom for a soul
Whom isn't ready to be set free
will only result is betrayal and tragedy
So dear lover come soon but not too soon
Know that I am waiting for you
Follow your heart and let your mind wonder
through Beaty of the world
And when your heart beats faster then ever and
your feet feel like running to complete all your
Endeavours
You'll feel a certain eager urge to find what's
yours
To find the lost soul once again in this man made
land of plastic paper and pollutants
My soul was once in the 7 heavens roaming
through endless green lands
Hand in hand with you
But now you have the task of finding me once
again
Only this time your being does not know
But soul never forgot me
So come find me in time you will
But for now just know I'm waiting for you and
only you dear lover .

Letting you go

Letting you go is the hardest part my dear
Loving you was easy
Just Like a breez over the East Sea;
But me and you
We just aren't meant to be
This world is so unfair
And this may be the unfairest way to say
Goodbye
But my departure now ,
will keep you away From me
so You fall as deeply for me
As I did for you
Our kits fly high but coming near yours meant
mine had to fall
I'm sorry
But I have to go
Yes I know
Letting you go
Isn't easy as you know
You think life for me is a breez
My heart is heavy and hurt
My soul reaps for you but my heart knows the
truth
My mind is confused but my soul keeps seeking
you

We aren't meant to be
But I wanted it to be
you and me
You and me forever like that
Why can't it be like that
I wish god will take mercy on me
My sorrow for my lost love is too deep
They say time will heal
But my pain isn't one that needs healing it needs
you and you are what makes me bleed
If me and you are meant to be
God will align Our destinies
Once again
But for now just know letting go wasn't easy for
me

Be happy

Be happy with yourself
Not with who you are
As who you are is preconceived notion of others
So my friend do not sit there in hast
Feel the world and feels it's waves
Feel the sea and it's Beaty
Feel what Allah made for you and me
This world is filled with the wonderful creation
of our creator
So why my friend
Why sit and waste the ticking of time
As the hourglass will pour
And time will be sure , to go
So be happy with yourself
As you only have yourself
In this world
Live and let live
Be
Not just to exist
Be
And be free , you have 15.77 billion acres of
land
The 7 seas all there for you and me

However if In search of happiness you are , your
Journey will only be for filled if happiness
resides within you
So my friend waste no more time
And be happy

Dear love

Like a drop in the ocean I'm searching for you
Dear love i feel like i will never find you
Is that how it's supposed to be
Feelings of emptiness and disperse
Crippling anxiety casted over my body
Dear love will i ever find you
In the search for my soul mate
Iv been so hurt and so broken
dates after dates
Heart breaks after breaks
Where do i find my true love
Who is my true love
I can't do this anymore
Me nor anyone will find love
As love Is like a drop in the ocean
A drop in the ocean a needle in a hay stack , but
to find love is even harder because I know what
I'm looking for may not exist
In a place so bless full of life
We taking take our blessings so light
I just want to feel happy and be alive

I am Palestine

I am Palestine
A place of Beaty And a place of grace
Misfortuned , displaced and seen as a disgrace
by the Israelis
My heart aces
More blood is on my streets
Then Blood running through my veins
My words are hushed and silenced
But my pain can not be contained
O the pain
Seeing a mother shot dead at point blank rang
O the pain
Seeing a child screaming it's mother's name
O the pain
As my people pray and they are shot dead in
vain
Does the world not see my suffering
A world of 7 billion eyes , ears and mouths
Why is ever eye blind
Ever ear deaf
And every mouth shut
My people are crying blood tear
Children that should be listening to nursery
rhymes at playtimes

Are now hearing the deafening sounds of bullet
shots and bomb drops ,
Young minds terrorised and tormented
Their futures stolen and replaced with trauma
and prison
Please I'm begging the world please don't let my
natives be muzzleid murdered
My men are all wounded
my women are all beaten
My children are all dying
my land is being stolen
Please world I'm crying here
I'm crying because I feel helpless
I can not alone stop the genocide of my Palestine
Share my word and share my shine
as i am innocent of any crime Western world
media can pain it lies
But god knows my heart is falling apart because
of their lies
Help me world
I am Palestine

Beating addiction

You came into my life a beautiful
Disguised lie
Looking for a fun time
I held onto you
But you sailed me so far into the sea
I couldn't see my way back
Now it's just you and me
Lonely looming through the sea
Yearning to know what it feels like to be unlost,
stable and steady
You're my friend and my foe
You know me and know that I can't let so
But I understand it was me who picked you
You're a sin so deadly you could kill me one day
But I still here puffing away
just feel some type of way
It's not easy for to let go
When comfort and peace Is what I know
When I puff puff puff
So it hard for me to let you go
Saying goodbye to you

Be happy

Be happy with yourself
Not with who you are
As who you are is preconceived notion of others
So my friend do not sit there in hast
Feel the world and feels it's waves
Feel the sea and it's Beaty
Feel what Allah made for you and me
This world is filled with the wonderful creation
of our creator
So why my friend
Why sit and waste the ticking of time
As the hourglass will pour
And time will be sure , to go
So be happy with yourself
As you only have yourself
In this world
Live and let live
Be
Not just to exist
Be
And be free , you have 15.77 billion acres of
land
The 7 seas all there for you and me

However if In search of happiness you are , your
Journey will only be for filled if happiness
resides within you
So my friend waste no more time
And be happy

Saying a girls goodbyes to the world

A series of events so extravagant and
extraordinary
At right time
and at the right place
to make a miracle that can never be replaced
Is the dream in any case,
From a seed to a pebble
From a pebble to being
from being being to a woman
Is where my journey of life ends
I am a women
I am a she
I am a being
i am me
But unfortunately
Reaching women-good
Strips a girl of any singularity ,Individuality and
dignity
Is a birth that every girl goes through
after her initial birth into this world

when taking off the blind fold
From her innocent child like face ,
to step into a world of men
A casket of misogyny and chauvinism
Is the parting gift we get.
At first thinking we are free to Rome this world
and to see all its glory and Beaty
In which we were conceived and brought up in ,
But the smile fades away and reminiscing
thoughts of my childhood linger
A childhood where I was told to reach for the
starts ,
To make a change
and to do what I want to do
And to make my own name ,
But The wicked cane of life teaches me fast
the only name I have for my own is the one that
Society can't over look ,
the name women
Which to me translates to
An adulthood where
I need a man to take me to the starts
.....
but O I don't want the stars anymore
I want to travel the sea and take in all its Beaty
But wait I am women
Why is that a problem you ask
What does that even mean
Where am I trying to go

Who am trying to be
When did I think it was okay to have such
ambitious ideas
So many Questions
my body is make of raw blood and flesh but I
feel transparent
why can people not see me for me
I live in a society where being a women means
nothing
if I don't have a man opaque
standing next to me.

Damaged

God gave us life
God is who we fear
But this life that I live
I don't hold it dear
Blessed with the blessing of my pears
this life that I live seems so senser
But I want to end it now
Before it's my turn
I'm greedy for grave
I'm Greedy for the grace
My eyes cry a river every day
In which it hopes to drown away its fears
But then comes another day
And I'm left feeling the same way
So I'm telling you
God gave us life
God is who we fear
So why can't I place my self near
Where I can see and hear god say
It's over dear
No need to fight anymore
Your way is clear now and I won't have to fear
the damage that was once done by the ones I
held dear
I want to live life not live in fear

So my eyes cry a river
hoping the end is nearer

I am Yemen

Dear world I am Yemen
A place so beautiful and full of life
Dim down by the hate and the constant fights
I plea and plea for the hate and glee in the heart
of the men who want to destroy me
Please Let me live
let my people see how beautiful tomorrow can
be
My soul is heavy and stained with the souls who
reap to see tomorrow
My sorrow is too deep i can not help my people
My land is distoyed and my children are left to
scving for food
Mothers and fathers deceased
I have no fight left in me
Please help me world
Please see me for me , I am a place of beauty
destroy by menkind and their greed
I can not sustain my people any longer
Please have it in your hearts to help me
So I can be the beautiful place that I once youse
to be
Leave the hate and glee in your hearts and get
together as nation to help me

Please give me and my people a chance , donate
to feed the mouths who are hungry because of
menkinds greeds ,
Know that I will never forget your favour
And I promise my people will give back to the
world what they once gave us ,
Humanity , love and peace

Dear earth

Green grass and endless land
Bright blue sky and the beauty of sea
They were such a blessing to me
You gave us life and to you we return
Scorching sun and worrying winters
Won't leave us alone
Dear earth please save us
Dear earth do you hear me
Dear earth I'm begging for your forgiveness
Let us live
Let us see all that you have to be
Let us see your beauty once again
Green grass and endless land
Bright blue sky and the beauty of the sea
Will be the miracles of the past
If we don't stand together and
Make the change that needs be
Don't take this lightly
You and me will be the last living legacies
To see this beauty
You and me are so greedy we write our name in
history as the wonderful murders of the beautiful
sea.

Dear black people

Dear black people
We are sorry ,
This apology is long overdue
Me
who has never experienced the pain and
discrimination of being black
Will never know what you've been through
But I am not blind ,I can see the pain that it
brings to you
when a world full of people turn a deaf ear to
your suffering and Prasue a narrative to
undermine your beautiful black ability's
We are sorry
Black is beautiful
Black is Beaty
Don't let the world hold you back from all that
you can be
Black is you and black is me

Loved you

I never intended to love you my dear,
However you were the match that
Sparked the first affairs of love
Kind, caring, carefree, love
Love that sounded sweeter,
then the birds tweeting melody in the morning
sky,
Love so big that the great Mount Everest would
shy away,
Love so deep that the deep sea would feel
shallow,
Determined to feel at the top of the world
These feelings quickly spiralled out of control,
What once sparked the fire of love,
Now is the fuel that drives you away from me
O why was I so stupid
To let you get so close me
O why was I so stupid
O why was I so stupid
I watched helplessly as you set fire to my heart
with the very match you ignited the flames of
love
But when I realised it was too late
The very hands that looked after you with love
,now want to hurt you

The very eyes that shed tears in worry of you ,
are crying for the truth
The soul that was so full of life now feels lost as
it believed love was the navigation to a better
life
Instead I'm left with wounds and scars from the
battles I fought through the journey of love,
And a trail of ash is left behind from the from
pieces of my heart you stole and burnt
What once seemed like
Kind caring carefree love
Was in fact
A plot in which my innocence was the weapon
you used to lure me into your trap
You said that loved me
But you never did

Who is Emma

A girl so beautiful and bright
Her inner light shines up the sky's at night
Her Beaty can not be contain
Her smile is like the sword that cuts through
pain
Her laughter ecos through my ear
As it's , beautiful melody travels through my
body
Who is Emma
Emma is an angel sent by god
Emma is a best friend
Emma is a sister
Emma is perfect in every way
People are flawed but my Emma she's just
Emma
Iv never felt no love like the love given by
Emma
She is comfort she is peace
She is all things great in a place where
The light of life is a mear flicker instead of a
flame
Emma is the hands that will hold you up in need
Emma is a vessel of good deeds and peace

Emma is a no ordinary girl
Her looks are killer
She's got a figure that'll put hourglass to shame
But most of all Emma is the girl who saved
my life
When the sharp edges of knife is what I consider
a friend
when everyone else gave up on me
Her purity and persistency to make me all that I
can be
Kept me alive even when disparity is all I could
see
She held my hand and lead me through every
struggle and vain
I felt like a empty shell drifting through the raft
of life without a meaning or purpose ready to
sink at anytime
But I was never alone Emma is the guidance that
bought me to shore
Emma is the guidance that taught me I am
capable of being loved and loving
Emma is the star in the dark night Sky when all
other stars are too scared to light up the way ,
Emma is that stare that shines brighter then any
other
Emma is my best friend and my soulmate
I hope you all find a Emma now that you know
who Emma is

A glimpse of hope in the life of those who are
strugglingPink & Blue

Pretty pink and pearly white board
blues and roaring read
Girls and boys are the same
You and I know who's bright
But it's only boys who get it right
Pink and pearly whites can only twirl
 but cannot fight

He & she

Mother makes me father makes me
At the end of the day I cannot be what I want to
be.
You see I plea and plea
I can only be another me and not what I want to
be
he who can write
he who can fight
he makes everything right
But I can't I am just a she
I simply cannot be a he
He and him can be exactly what they want to be
But I have to stay at home and be a she
World is infinite and endless opportunity
But me all I am is just a she
Can be he
he can be me
he can be exactly what he wants to be
But I have to stay at home and be a she
a she who has a voice
she who is it deafen blind but the world does not
see all that I have to be to them I am just as she.

www.ingramcontent.com/pod-product-compliance
Lightning Source LLC
LaVergne TN
LVHW021342200726
843509LV00014B/2635